YOUR KNOWLEDGE HAS VALUE

Nataliya Gudz

Hard Eurosceptics can never be convinced of the case for European integration - or can they?

GRIN Verlag

Bibliografische Information der Deutschen Nationalbibliothek:

Die Deutsche Bibliothek verzeichnet diese Publikation in der Deutschen National-
bibliografie; detaillierte bibliografische Daten sind im Internet über http://dnb.d-
nb.de/ abrufbar.

Imprint:

Copyright © 2007 GRIN Verlag GmbH
Druck und Bindung: Books on Demand GmbH, Norderstedt Germany
ISBN: 978-3-640-18429-3

This book at GRIN:

http://www.grin.com/en/e-book/116371/hard-eurosceptics-can-never-be-convinced-
of-the-case-for-european-integration

GRIN - Your knowledge has value

Der GRIN Verlag publiziert seit 1998 wissenschaftliche Arbeiten von Studenten, Hochschullehrern und anderen Akademikern als eBook und gedrucktes Buch. Die Verlagswebsite www.grin.com ist die ideale Plattform zur Veröffentlichung von Hausarbeiten, Abschlussarbeiten, wissenschaftlichen Aufsätzen, Dissertationen und Fachbüchern.

Visit us on the internet:

http://www.grin.com/

http://www.facebook.com/grincom

http://www.twitter.com/grin_com

NATOLIN (WARSAW) CAMPUS
Master in European Interdisciplinary Studies

Hard Eurosceptics can never be convinced of the case for European integration —or can they?

Nataliya GUDZ
EU Institutions, Politics and Policies
Word Count: 3084

Academic Year 2007-2008

*"Each time we must choose between Europe and the open sea,
we shall always choose the open sea",*

1

I. Introduction

Signed fifty years ago, the Treaty of Rome proclaimed an "ever closer union"[1] by "establishing a common market and progressive approximation of the economic policies of member states"[2]. This approximation had, however, a negative side effect – opposition to market integration, and after the sequence of enlargements – ardent resistance to any further European integration. Moreover, since the Maastricht Treaty, Eurosceptics have exploited a new battleground: 'defence of national community'[3] in response to the erosion of national sovereignty and to the heightened job insecurity caused by market unification and liberalization process.

As enlargement process was taking its course, Euroscepticism grew into a potent feature of the political landscape across the EU, by not only shaking confidence in the process of further enlargement, but also 'provoking several attempts to re-theorize the process of European integration'[4]. Thus, for example, 'soft eurosceptics' (definition proposed by Paul Taggart and Aleks Szczerbiak[5]) opposed to the "EU's current or future planned trajectory based on the future extension of competencies"[6], whereas the main objective of their 'hard counterparts' was "tantamount to being de facto opposed to EU membership"[7].

In this paper we'll try to analyse a phenomenon of hard Euroscepticism in the European Union by presenting Danish and British cases. We'll demonstrate that sometimes hard Eurosceptic parties can be convinced of the case for European integration, despite their ardent anti-EU positions.

---

[1] Preamble, Treaty of Rome
[2] Art. 2, Treaty of Rome
[3] Hooghe, Lisbet, and Marks, Gary, *Sources of Euroscepticism*, Acta Politica, 2007, 42, p. 121
[4] Ibid., p. 119
[5] Taggart, Paul, and Szczerbiak, Aleks, *The Party Politics of Euroscepticism in EU Member and Candidate States*, ECPR Papers, Turin, March, 2002, p. 4
[6] Ibid., p. 5
[7] Ibid., p. 4

II. Eurosceptics yesterday and today: changes and stability

Coined in the British political and media usage in the late 1970s and used as a synonym for the older 'anti-marketeer'[8] to describe popular British opposition towards European integration, in our days Euroscepticism is vividly present not only in the UK, but also in other parts of the enlarged Europe. The UK, Sweden, and Denmark, for example, declined full participation in the Economic and Monetary Union. Non-members (Norway, Iceland and especially, the German-speaking cantons in Switzerland) were reluctant to expand ties with the EU or accept membership. In the recent years, hard Euroscepticism has grown in the new member states in Central and Eastern Europe (particular, in Poland, Hungary and Czech Republic), as a trend for preserving national sovereignty in the face of European integration with the reference to particular collective national identities and symbols.

Exactly the issue of preservation of national identity and sovereignty was a principal element in the rhetoric of hard Eurosceptics in the Nordic countries and Britain. Notwithstanding the negative feelings towards the EU, some political parties in these countries could manage to find compromise and to adopt their political agenda to the current situation.

2.1. Nordic countries: Denmark

Supporting an old Nordic tradition to trade without entering into the binding treaties with other states and being devoted to their neutral political position, Sweden, Denmark, Norway, Iceland, and Finland have historically resisted the idea of European unity, being absent at the creation of the Treaty of Rom, but eventually joined the EFTA. Due to "the growing interdependence of European political economies and the changing distribution of military power, requiring the reassessment of economic and security policies"[9], in the mid-1980s the Nordic states had to alter substantially the nature of their relations with the EEC pursuing closer cooperation. Beside Iceland and Norway,

---

[8] Harsen, Robert, *A dual exceptionalism: British and French patterns of Euroscepticism in wider comparative perspective*, Centre for the Study of Democratic Government, European Research Group, 2005, p. 1 (http://erg.politics.ox.ac.uk/projects/national_identity/papers.asp, assessed 22.10.2007)
[9] Ingebritsen, Christine, *The Nordic States and European Unity*, Ithaca, NY: Cornell University Press, 1998, p.12

3

which are the most resistant to joining the EU, other Nordic states have shifted their economic and security preferences from the national welfare states to the European level.

For instance, Denmark - known to be one of the hardest Eurosceptic states – was the first among the Nordic States to join the EEC (1972). Though quoting Eric Einhorn, "when the Danes joined the European Community, they did so with their purses – not their hearts"[10], during the first decade in the EC the single market was developing with many advantages for the Danish economy, particularly its agricultural sector. Moreover, the Danish support for membership has also steadily risen: from 42 % in 1973 to 57% in 2003[11]. And in 2003 Denmark scored "higher positive attitudes than traditionally pro-EU countries such as Belgium"[12].

After a rather overwhelming support at the referendum on the Single European Act (1986) and controversial confirmation at the highest level by then prime minister Poul Schlüter that "the union was stone dead"[13], the Danes became more positively inclined towards additional institutional changes on the EU level and further empowerment of the European Parliament. However, despite the evident economic profit from the internal market and the Danish enthusiasm to turn the EC into more than just a "pragmatic acquaintance"[14], in 1992 the Danes rejected the TEU by a narrow margin (50,7% against and 49,3% in favour)[15]. Moreover, this referendum gave birth to another hard Eurosceptic single-issue movement (*the June Movement*), just as *The People's Movement against the EU* emerged as direct response to Danish membership in the EC in 1972.

The Danish dissatisfaction with the EU became also apparent during the referendum on Amsterdam Treaty in 1998. Despite the yes-campaign initiated by then Prime Minister Nyrup Rasmussen on the economic benefits from joining the single currency and the

[10] Ibid., p. 11-12
[11] Sorensen, Catharina, *Danish and British popular Euroscepticism compared: a sceptical assessment of the concept*, Danish Institute for Internal Studies, DIIS Working paper 2004, p. 7
[12] Ibid., p. 7
[13] Ibid., p. 13
[14] Ibid., p. 13
[15] Ingebritsen, Christine, *The Nordic States and European Unity*, Ithaca, NY: Cornell University Press, 1998, p. 124

necessity "to vote with their heads"[16], a post-referendum survey showed that economic arguments had a significant impact only on 16% of the electorate.

In the recent years, the Danish Eurosceptics are steadily coming back to the ardent oppositionist roots. Using immigration and asylum issues and underlying general perception of any EU integration as a threat to Danish integrity, national identity and sovereignty, they are advancing with this "scenario, which most yes-voters as well as no-voters would oppose"[17].

2.2. Britain

Geographically situated on the periphery of Europe, with the feelings of remoteness from the mainland, Britain – as an island fortress – has always underlined its sense of exceptionalism, 'cultural otherness'[18], or 'Britishness'[19]. This idea of British exceptionalism finds ready parallels in the cases of the Nordic countries or Switzerland – where similar discourses have emerged, aiming "to defend a distinctive *'Nordic Model'* or the *'Sonderfall Schweiz'* from what are perceived to be 'homogenising' influences of European integration"[20].

For this very reason, Britain's reluctance to give up any of its sovereignty is explained with "reference to its uniqueness, and this, in turn, is related to both its island tradition and the antiquity of its institutions[21]. British independence and 'superiority feeling' towards Europe whose "institutions swept away by wars and revolutions"[22], British overseas orientation as the centre of the "pink empire, covering two-fifth of the globe"[23]

---

[16] Sorensen, Catharina, *Danish and British popular Euroscepticism compared: a sceptical assessment of the concept*, Danish Institute for Internal Studies, DIIS Working paper 2004, p. 15

[17] Ibid., p. 16

[18] Harmsen, Robert, *A dual exceptionalism: British and French patterns of Euroscepticism in wider comparative perspective*, Centre for the Study of Democratic Government, European Research Group, 2005, p. 8 (http://erg.politics.ox.ac.uk/projects/national_identity/papers.asp, assessed 24.10.2007)

[19] Baker, David, *E with much less U: or No more E or U? British Eurosceptic exceptionalism after enlargement*, Centre for the Study of Democratic Government, European Research Group, 2005, p. 4 (http://erg.politics.ox.ac.uk/projects/national_identity/papers.asp, assessed 23.10.2007)

[20] Harmsen, Robert, *A dual exceptionalism: British and French patterns of Euroscepticism in wider comparative perspective*, Centre for the Study of Democratic Government, European Research Group, 2005, p. 4 (http://erg.politics.ox.ac.uk/projects/national_identity/papers.asp, assessed 24.10.2007)

[21] Musolff, Andrea, Good, Colin, Points, Petra, Wittlinger, Ruth, Hants, Aldershot, *Attitudes towards Europe, Language in the unification process*, England; Burlington, VT: Ashgate, 2001, p. 8

[22] Ibid., p. 8

[23] Sorensen, Catharina, *Danish and British popular Euroscepticism compared: a sceptical assessment of the concept*, Danish Institute for Internal Studies, DIIS Working paper 2004, p. 19

and its key concept of parliamentary sovereignty and indivisibility, made the strong base for the emergence of hard Eurosceptic discourse in Britain. The mixture of all these factors made Britain stand aside in the first phase of European integration in the 1950s, as Churchill in 1953 stated: "We are with Europe but not of it. We are linked but not comprised. We are interested and associated, but not absorbed. We do not intend to be merged in a European federal system"[24].

However, in early 1960s a new generation of Conservatives turned round to Europe by making an application to join EU in 1961, which was rejected two years later by De Gaulle who considered Britain to be "insular, maritime, and profoundly differing from the other states of the Continent"[25]. The British application was vetoed again by De Gaulle in 1967, when Macmillan's government made a repeated application for the EC accession, breaking up with an old tradition of British exceptionalism and betraying national sovereignty that would not be lost in a united Europe but just 'pooled'[26].

Such a U-turn of the governing party didn't imply its conversion into enthusiastic Europeans. Considering costs and benefits of the EC accession, the Conservatives needed the European Community as 'economic panacea' helping the British economy to overcome many of its problems without "restoring to a radical and painful domestic economic overhaul"[27]. Additionally, such British openness to the European Community was also based on its trauma by the loss of British global power as the process of decolonisation accelerated. Therefore "the Conservatives essentially saw the EC as a fledging, young organisation which British leadership could shape and mould"[28]. From 1967 onwards they have argued that Britain should be at the "heart of Europe to influence events and not standing on the sidelines"[29]. British reassurances of its serious intentions and steady French acknowledgement of the need to counterbalance the growing weight of West Germany, finally led to the British accession in 1972.

---

[24] Holmes, Martin, *European Integration. Scope and Limits*, Houndmills, Basingstoke, Hampshire ; New York : Palgrave, 2001, p. 15
[25] Sorensen, Catharina, *Danish and British popular Euroscepticism compared: a sceptical assessment of the concept*, Danish Institute for Internal Studies, DIIS Working paper 2004, p. 17
[26] Musolff, Andrea, Good, Colin, Points, Petra, Wittlinger, Ruth, Hants, Aldershot, *Attitudes towards Europe, Language in the unification process*, England; Burlington, VT: Ashgate, 2001, p. 11
[27] Holmes, Martin, *European Integration. Scope and Limits*, Houndmills, Basingstoke, Hampshire ; New York : Palgrave, 2001, p. 17
[28] Ibid., p. 16
[29] Ibid., p. 22

Unlike the Danish case, there was no prior referendum on membership in the UK. Three years later, however, "an overwhelming 2-to-1 majority decided … that Britain was to stay in 'European Community (the Common Market)', as the referendum question called it"[30] in spite of Labour Party's opposition to the EC.

Since its accession in 1972 Britain was considered to be the most sceptic and ambivalent among the member states, that always fought for its sensitive national interests with such ardour and skills that succeeded to obtain infamous economic rebate, opt-outs from the single currency and social policy, and weakening the supranational elements of new treaty proposals at IGCs. All these elements have shaped the invaluable heritage of discrepancies, left by Conservatives to their followers.

Despite Margaret Thatcher's ardent "No. No. No."[31] on federal Europe during her first years as Prime Minister and her uncompromising style and stubbornness as a politician ("The lady is not for turning" and "TINA" - There is no alternative)[32], the prospect of giving the free market a European dimension made Margaret Thatcher a keen supporter of the Single Market project. Her preoccupation was, firstly, a battle for a better budget deal for Britain (getting 'her money back'), and secondly, promotion of qualified majority voting (QMV) as a tactic to overcome protectionist opposition to the single market. Further Thatcher advocated the core idea of hard Conservative Eurosceptics to defence sovereignty and to oppose any federalist attempts. In her famous Bruges speech, Thatcher proposed a wider, decentralised, outward-looking democratic Europe of independent, freely-trading and cooperating nations, opposing it to centralised, unaccountable, federal Europe of Delors: "The European Community is *one* manifestation of that European identity. But it is not the only one"[33].

This idea of preserving British sovereignty at any price made John Major confront the split in the Conservative party (Maastricht Rebels) on the issue of Maastricht Treaty in 1992. Being torn apart between the Thatcherites ('A treaty too far'[34]) and his own

---

[30] Sorensen, Catharina, *Danish and British popular Euroscepticism compared: a sceptical assessment of the concept*, Danish Institute for Internal Studies, DIIS Working paper 2004, p. 17

[31] Musolff, Andrea, Good, Colin, Points, Petra, Wittlinger, Ruth, Hants, Aldershot, *Attitudes towards Europe, Language in the unification process*, England; Burlington, VT: Ashgate, 2001, p. 26

[32] Ibid., p. 28

[33] http://www.brugesgroup.com/about/columnists.live?person=36, accessed 10.11.2007

[34] Baker, David, Seawright, David, *Britain for and against Europe: British politics and the question of European integration*, Oxford: Clarendon Press ; New York : Oxford University Press, 1998, p. 37

commitment to a 'Europe of nation states'[35], Major skilfully contrived a compromise between two parts of his party. He negotiated three qualifications to appease Eurosceptics. "The word *federal* was deleted from the Treaty. Britain was exempted from the Social Charta, which Thatcher had once characterized as Marxist. A decision in relation to monetary union was deferred for approval by the British Parliament until Stage III commenced"[36]. Moreover, by negotiating opt-outs for the single currency and social chapter, a temporary political peace was bought at the expense of the national interest in that "in order to prove his credentials Major had to agree to greater European integration. He had to endorse everything Mrs Thatcher had said NO to, including EMU"[37]. By leading his country toward a fundamental renegotiation of Britain's relationship with continental Europe, manifesting strong sentiments in favour of European integration and "putting Britain at the heart of Europe"[38], John Major concerned Britain to be unconditional member of the EU in which the benefits outweighed the costs.

In comparison to the Conservatives' ambivalent behaviour regarding EU, the Labourists – originally opposed to membership in 1972 – were forced by Tony Blair's EU-enthusiasm ("I am a passionate pro-European. I always have been"[39]) in 2006 to support a "multi-million pound propaganda war to force the British people to love the European Union and Brussels bureaucrats"[40]. Unlike Blair, his follower, Gordon Brown, is now turning back to 'British exceptionalism' by restating the importance of British interests and values, neglected by Blair in his attempts to join the euro.

2.3. Representation in the European Parliament

In the mid-90s, still believing into the possible change of the EC integration, members of the Danish and British hard Eurosceptic parties were elected to the European Parliament in order to influence the development of Europe within the EC institutions. By establishing EDD group (*Europe of Democracies and Diversities*) in cooperation

---

[35] Ibid., p. 37
[36] Holmes, Martin, *European Integration. Scope and Limits*, Houndmills, Basingstoke, Hampshire ; New York : Palgrave, 2001, p. 30
[37] Ibid, p. 30
[38] Ibid., p. 48
[39] http://www.britischebotschaft.de/en/news/items/050623.htm, accessed 16.11.2007
[40] http://www.dailymail.co.uk/pages/live/articles/news/news.html?in_article_id=420090&in_page_id=1770, accessed 16.11.2007

with other hard anti-EU parties, the Eurosceptics were entrapped in their own trap. "A high level of compromise has been necessary for a single-issue and hard Eurosceptics to reach the minimum thresholds for group formation, given their heterogeneous origins"[41]. Moreover, to gain access to resources and to participate in the decision-making of the European Parliament (committees, rapporteurs, etc.), Eurosceptics had to make alliances, sometimes not always with those who shared a similar perspective on integration. Not very reluctant to compromises, the members of the EDD group were under-represented in the European parliamentary hierarchy due to their "self-elimination and self-exclusion"[42].

Nevertheless, the efforts in consensus management and compromise-finding in the EP helped some hard Eurosceptics to change their ardent opposition to the EU to a softer position, based on a critical observation of the European enlargement process. This shift gained them a better level of institutionalisation and coherence on the European level that later was successfully implemented also on the national levels.

III. Conclusions

The present paper analysed behaviour of the hard Eurosceptics in Denmark and Britain. Established already before accession to the EC, the Eurosceptic parties in these member states proved to be very active, always putting onto agenda the burning questions of the European integration. However, sooner or later, all of them acknowledged the undoubtful benefits of being 'in'. Furthermore it provided them with a possibility to try to change the European Union from within. For instance, participation in the European Parliament turned out to be a litmus test for hard Eurosceptics who were forced to cooperate, to find compromise and to build coalitions (so unnatural to their radical roots) in order to gain some power in the decision-making of the EP. Gradually abandoning their hard concepts on Euroscepticism, the anti-EU parties moved slowly to softer positions, because it guaranteed them more influence in the agenda-setting and the decision-making process either on the European or on the national level. Despite this

---

[41] Giacomo, Benedetto, *Euroscepticism and the failure of "blackmail" power in the European Parliament*, the ECPR Joint Sessions, Torino, 2002, p. 8
[42] Ibid., p. 22

'softening', some of the former hard Eurosceptics still consider the EU to be a source of threat to national identity, sovereignty and, thus, stability.

As the European Union is widening and deepening, it is, at the same time, becoming more distant and less comprehensible for its citizens, and it's concurrently provoking more critical approach to the European integration. Therefore its future destiny will be counterbalanced between hopes and doubts, since the latter leads to a possible truth, as a former Danish Foreign Minister, Per Stig Moller, once stated: "I doubt, therefore I am a European"[43].

---

[43] Sorensen, Catharina, *Danish and British popular Euroscepticism compared: a sceptical assessment of the concept*, Danish Institute for Internal Studies, DIIS Working paper 2004, p. 2